TOP TIPS
—— FOR TEACHING ——
SUAVE WORDS

Top Tips for Teaching Suave Words

Written by Ros Wilson.
Edited and proof read by Richard Robinson.
Cover and design by Dan Wilson.

Published by P and R Education Ltd.
83 Haigh Lane, Haigh, Wakefield, West Yorkshire, S75 4DA.
Directors – Ben Pilmer and Richard Robinson.

www.RosWilsonEd.com
hello@RosWilsonEd.com
Twitter: @RosBigWriting
Facebook and Instagram: RosWilsonEd

ISBN: 978-1-8381761-2-9.

First published in 2023. First edition.

About Ros

Ros entered the teaching profession in 1965 and has served continuously in education. She has wide experience in the field, including: working with pupils with SEND; working with pupils with EAL; Senior Leadership; Head of large primary department overseas; Local Authority Adviser; Primary Strategy Manager; Independent Consultant; Advanced Skills Teacher Assessor; Ofsted Inspector; Curriculum Designer and author of *The Creative Curriculum*; Creator and Author of *Big Writing* and associated texts (Oxford University Press).

More recently, Ros has worked part time as a consultant and as a guest speaker at events. She has published several books since 2019 and developed the *Talk:Write* programme.

Ros has lived and worked overseas, including in The Caribbean and Qatar. Her hobbies are writing and talking.

To find out more, visit:
www.RosWilsonEd.com
or find us on Twitter, Facebook or Instagram.

Acknowledgements

Thank you to Mike Hindle, Rob Potts, Sam Rennison and Michelle Wraith for reading and giving feedback on an early draft of this book.

Thank you to Ania @not_her_1104, Haroon @schoolimprover, Mike @hindle_mike, Lisa @Lisibo, Philip @Scottcog, Rehana @MrsRYasmeen and Tbarak @Tbarakmahar for their support on Twitter with word translations.

Sam Rennison, Deputy Head, Parklands Primary School
What an absolutely inspirational read. Vocabulary is key and I believe that working as a whole school, introducing these new ambitious suave words, will enable our children to compete later in life with their peers.

Rob Potts, Author of *The Caring Teacher*, Whole School Recovery Lead
I was blown away by how effective it is at not only developing vocabulary but also instilling confidence and a love of language. Moreover, by avoiding the temptation to overload the children and focusing instead on embedding vocabulary through regular repetition and fun activities, this book ensures that the results are sustained and children are inspired to explore and play with language with confidence and flair.

Mike Hindle, Headteacher, Kings College International School, Wuxi, China
This book is a really welcome support tool for the development of high quality talk and writing in our classrooms. With the knowledge that scaffolded talk opportunities and the promotion of a rich and varied vocabulary increase children's levels of confidence, communication, writing voice and ability to flourish, teachers are constantly looking for ideas that are proven to work in the classroom. The wealth of ideas presented in this book are immediately usable and simple, as well as being hugely enjoyable.

Contents

Introduction

This book is a quick and easy guide for teachers of all pupils aged 5 to 13 learning in English speaking schools. It is intended to give simple, fun and highly effective strategies for the teaching of sophisticated vocabulary which we call **suave words.**

Pro-active teaching of suave words is an extremely important aspect of teaching language in the classroom.

Increasingly, Early Years leaders and teachers are reporting that many children are entering nursery and even reception with a significant lack of vocabulary. Amongst the most important priorities for these children must be the expansion of their basic vocabulary and a gradual increase in exposure to a more enriched range of words. This is addressed through enjoyable activities, discussion in free play, light-hearted group story and discussions. As children mature, games and activities are included in all teaching across the curriculum.

The teaching and learning ideas in this book apply to the teaching of all vocabulary. Having a wide vocabulary is not the same as having a sophisticated vocabulary, although it would ideally include the latter.

Having a full and rich vocabulary is empowering for all of us in both spoken and written communication. Teaching suave words is not just about teaching long and complex words that many may not know. Rather, it is about having a wide range of choices, that include simple but sophisticated words, to avoid potential repetition and to enrich text. Thus, all teachers should be looking constantly for opportunities to use synonyms in their taught input, making links and explaining usages.

Many parents today have less time than ever to sit down and chat with their children, let alone to read with them, tell stories, play games and generally interact in the many ways that teach children the crucial skills of oral communication. Teachers report having children start school aged three, four or even five with a much narrower range of vocabulary than seen historically, and in some instances a significant number of school starters are not yet speaking in complete sentences. If children can't speak in sentences, they won't write in them (even when they are ready to write). Addressing a restricted vocabulary or a lack of language skills is a key part of raising standards across the curriculum.

In addition, many children enter English curriculum schools today with little or no English due to relocation from other countries, or as a result of parents in other countries choosing to have their children educated in the English education system. As they develop their linguistic skills in English, they also absorb the enriched new vocabulary that their peers are learning – indeed, many will already know similar words in their first language.

Success in secondary and higher education is greatly impacted by language skills, both in written and oral examinations. In addition, success at interviews is often directly affected by the interviewee's ability to articulate their interests, knowledge and understanding relevant to the opportunity. Thus, the pro-active teaching of vocabulary enhances future life opportunities.

Whatever the age, whatever the need, this book will enable teachers to expand their pupils' vocabulary confidently and with clear understanding of meaning and application in their ever-widening repertoire.

The teaching of suave words and a generally wider vocabulary is empowering and makes the skill of writing so much more rewarding and enjoyable. Many of your pupils may have already met many of the words you teach, but they are not yet conscious of the language they have, and they do not **seek it out** in their subconscious when they are writing.

When we teach children a wider and richer vocabulary, the aim is not to impose a more elitist language on them. Rather, it is to empower them with a wider range of choices and further enable them to develop their own unique **voice**. Far from demanding that all pupils use all the words we choose to teach, we seek to see preferences that will express each pupil's individuality.

I love writing. It is my number one interest and always has been. I have always believed that it is because I am lucky enough to **have the words**. I grew up the youngest in an impoverished single-parent family. My mother took in university students for income (it was before the days of benefits and pensions). She was cooking and cleaning for eleven of us most of the time. These were the days before TV. We spent most of our evenings at the kitchen table discussing, debating and arguing. I got the words!

Words are power!
Give your pupils the words and they too will have the power.

The fundamental principles behind the teaching of suave words is one of the five key elements of our Talk:Write programme. This programme is split into sections that can be taught totally independently and thus teachers can introduce elements one at a time or only ever implement the one most needed in their school.

Many teachers have started the programme with the suave word element and report great successes with that alone. It is for this reason that we have released this guide to improving literacy and oracy skills through the teaching of suave words.

We hope you will enjoy the fun of this initiative and see the immediate impact it has on pupils' achievement.

SECTION ONE
TOP TIPS AND ADVICE

What Are Suave Words?

A **suave word** is our fun name for sophisticated words or ambitious vocabulary. We chose this name because we wanted to use a word that none of the children are likely to know already and that is short and easy to learn.

When first teaching the spelling of **suave**, it may be useful to do so in parallel with the word **language** – which the children will know, and which uses the same *u* sounding like a *w*.

We should regard the teaching of suave words in English, and across the curriculum, as being similar to the teaching of times tables in mathematics.

They are basic tools to enable greater success in a wider range of the subject's requirements. The teaching of these words should become part of the daily and weekly routines of a school.

Why Use Suave Words?

- **Suave** means charming. In that sense it is usually applied to people. However, it also means sophisticated, elegant and debonair – a perfect description for many wonderful words in the English language.
- Suave words are usually words that children do not regularly meet in their normal daily exposure to reading, listening to stories, watching or listening to programmes or in conversation at home or in school. They would need to be reading fairly sophisticated books and holding regular sophisticated discussions to learn this type of word through those behaviours.

- Suave words can be any part of speech. Thus, by Year 6 we may hear:
  - common nouns, e.g. **angst** instead of **anxious**.
  - verbs, e.g. **devoured** instead of **ate**.
  - adjectives, e.g. **tasteful** instead of **nice**.
  - adverbs, e.g. **swiftly** instead of **fast**.
  - prepositions, e.g. **beneath** instead of **under**.
- Suave words do not have to be long or complicated – they just have to be words that are less usually heard or read. This is why our suave word of the week resources are most often words of only one or at most two syllables, making them easier to learn and use. Having only one syllable does not make these words any less impactful when heard in speech or read in writing.
- Suave words are words that most children may never learn if a teacher does not teach them.
- Suave words are ambitious but appropriate for children of the age they are taught to. Only the class teacher knows what their children are ready for. Our range of suave words is diverse so there are always appropriate choices.
- Children aged seven upwards may cope with longer and more complex words, in particular:
  - if the word interests or excites them,
  - if the word is a composite of short words they already know e.g. **sometimes** or **headlong**,
  - if the word involves a known prefix or suffix on a root word they already know, such as **hurtful**, **misplaced** or **distressed**.
- *Suave word plus* is our term for longer and more complex vocabulary for children aged seven and above, if they are ready. These are words that very often have three or more syllables and are completely new to the children, such as **mortified** and **industrious** *(see page 63)*.

Our free suave word resources can be downloaded from our website.
www.RosWilsonEd.com/free

Why Should We Teach Suave Words?

Over many years of pro-active teaching of vocabulary, it has often been said that teachers should not have to consciously teach ambitious words. Rather, that children should *discover* them for themselves through reading. Vocabulary is not language per se. It is the building blocks to construct language and increase its effectiveness.

Good quality, pro-active teaching includes discovery, exploration, investigation and experimentation of both provided text and pupil-generated text. All are contexts for exploring the use of new and interesting words.

Research shows that most children require up to 12 exposures – in different contexts – to a new and challenging word to fully understand and use it.

Meeting a word once or twice through talk or reading will not naturally enrich the retained vocabulary of most children.

The other essential features of language will also continue to be taught through the school's agreed systems.

Benefits of Teaching Suave Words

- Suave words will enrich children's speech and writing, when used appropriately.
- Pupils will be empowered by an increased choice of vocabulary.
- Pupils will be more effective communicators.
- The teaching of suave words raises standards for pupils.

- Children do not regularly meet many suave words in everyday activities, so they rarely learn them.
- Children need multiple exposures to words to embed them. An intentional, curriculum-wide approach will greatly enhance pupils' chances of expanding their vocabulary.
- Having a rich and varied vocabulary can help to enhance a child's later life chances. For example, in passing higher exams, which are often influenced by the standard and quality of expression, and in interviews and presentations.
- The more they hear and use a new word, the faster children will learn it and the better they will retain it and fully understand how to use it. This confirms that new and flexible approaches to teaching new vocabulary are needed.

Remember

- Not all children will learn all the words. That's OK! Trust your judgement. As long as all children know and use some suave words, the objective is achieved.
- Suggested ages are approximate. If you think your children are ready, go for it. If you think they are not, hold back.
- Reading is essential for children and enriches their lives. It should be a special time in the curriculum. Although it is not the best vehicle for teaching new words, it provides a great source for new vocabulary that can then be taught using the suave word activities. It also provides an engrossing forum for enhancing understanding of the use of new vocabulary in different contexts.
- Teaching words alone is not teaching language, but words are the building blocks of language. As soon as children can construct simple oral sentences, we advocate introducing strategies to broaden their vocabulary in ways that are simple and enjoyable.

How Do We Teach Suave Words?

The teaching of suave words does not require changes to the daily timetable or dedicated lessons. The initial launch of a new word usually takes between 10 and 15 minutes. It may take place at the start or end of an English lesson, or in a lesson for another subject if use of the new word could complement current learning in the subject.

The launch should be repeated three times or more over the first week, across the curriculum, and then quick games and activities should be used for full familiarisation, learning and confidence. These activities usually take around five minutes each and may take place in any subject or between lessons as a brain break.

There are a wide range of resources to support the launch of each new suave word on our website.
www.RosWilsonEd.com/free

The teaching of a new suave word is a pro-active endeavour that should be planned ahead. When introducing a new word, always use the visual, written form as you say the word clearly at least three times. Then give the definition, explaining the differences if it commonly has more than one meaning. Always give one or more examples for its use.

Modifications to this advice on introducing new words may need to be made to enable pupils with particular needs to have full access to the learning.

Decisions on whether to expand initial teaching of a new word to include use of common prefixes and suffixes should be made by the teacher, based on the age, understanding and readiness of the children. It can be more effective to embed the new word first before exploring expansions. If the expansions are already known to the children, they may be suggesting them from the start.

Do not use pronouns in place of the word when children are meeting it for the first few times. Use the target word repeatedly in your introductory teaching to embed the pronunciation and structure.

Instead of:

> **Toil** is a truly suave word to use. I want to hear you use it when you are talking. I want to see it in your writing.

Say:

> **Toil** is a truly suave word to use. I want to hear you use **toil** when you are talking. I want to see the word **toil** in your writing.

As with all teaching, some decisions about the use of the advice in this book must remain the jurisdiction of the teacher. This includes at what age to launch the teaching of suave words. In some cases, children aged four to seven may only meet the new words and have their meaning explained so that they can enjoy the assemblies and activities they are present for. In other cases, children from four or five upwards may start playing the games and using the words in their talk and writing from first exposure to them.

School Launch of the Suave Word of the Week

- The new suave word of the week should preferably be launched on the first day of the school week.
- Suggested suave words are published on our website and the new suave word is posted on social media each week.

- The new suave word of the week is usually launched in assembly to the whole school, key stage or year by the head or a senior leader *(see page 35)*.
- The word should be introduced and explained, then used in one or two sentences to exemplify. The whole assembly could then play one of the simple games or could make up a sentence with the word in, with the child sitting next to them. The word will then be reintroduced later in individual classes.
- The assembly might finish with the suave word school champions competition *(see page 35)*.
- Older children may have a second suave word each week (we call these **suave word plus**), usually introduced from the middle of the week onwards. This may be more complex and is often relevant to subject matter under study; e.g. **anxiety** or **anguish** when studying the fate of two of Henry VIII's wives or the animal population of a forest when logging takes place.

Class Launch of the Suave Word of the Week

- Write the suave word in large, clear letters on the whiteboard or flip chart.
- All read the word together three times.
- Give the meaning and explain it. Give examples of use. The teacher should decide whether to focus on the most common or useful meaning to start with, or whether all meanings should be explained at once, based on the word difficulty and their knowledge of their class.
- All repeat the word and meaning together three or more times.
- All spell the word out loud together three times. If spelling is not regular, or is complex, it will need to be taught pro-actively using the school's agreed method for teaching complex spellings.
- Model use of the word in a sentence. This may be linked to current learning.

- Play **make me up** *(see page 39)*. All children make up oral sentences about different stimuli given in rapid succession, and then share answers. This could be in twos or threes if children need support or confidence to start with.
- All children are encouraged to write two or three sentences that include the word immediately or as soon as possible after starting to learn it, and to use it orally.

Model for Teaching the New Suave Word of the Week

Teacher: Our new suave word of the week is **angst**. Look everyone, here is **angst** on the wall. Isn't **angst** a strange looking word? Let's all read **angst** together three times. Ready?

All: angst angst angst

Teacher: Angst means anxious or worried or full of anxiety. Can anyone say what **angst** means? That's right – **angst** means worry or worried about something. A person who is feeling **angst** is worried about something. Let's all say **angst** and **angst's** meaning – worry or worried – together three times. Ready?

All: Angst means worry or worried; **angst** means worry or worried; **angst** means worry or worried.

Teacher: Now let's all spell and say **angst** together three times. Ready?

All: a n g s t **angst**; a n g s t **angst**; a n g s t **angst**.

Teacher: Now I am going to use the word **angst** in a sentence. Ready? I was feeling **angst** about teaching this new suave word today. How was I feeling everyone?

All: Worried.

Teacher: Good, now let's play *make me up*. Please all make up your own sentence and share it with your partner. Well done. I really liked Sofia's. She said she is feeling **angst** about being in the school play. There is no need for that Sofia. You will be excellent. Well done, everyone. We will all start geography after lunch by writing three sentences about which animals in the rainforest might be feeling **angst**, and why. Now it is time for PE, so let's all change quietly.

Teaching a Suave Word Across the Week

- If it is a whole-school or key-stage initiative, the head or a senior leader launches a whole-school suave word of the week in assembly at the start of the week *(see page 35)*.
- The class teacher launches or relaunches the new word in the English lesson. It may only be in the introduction or plenary.
- Very young children may just repeat the word and say the meaning. They may *spot* the word when the teacher and other adults use it. It is an introduction for them. They are not necessarily expected to learn or use it yet, although often some do.
- All children are given the new word as suave word homework *(see page 32)*.
- Staff create as many opportunities as possible to use the word in all lessons across the first week of launch.

- All children revisit the introductory stage *(see page 14)* at least twice more during the week. This may not be in English lessons. If the word is relevant to an aspect of the wider curriculum, a session can take place in that subject.
- The activities and examples used are changed with each relaunch.
- All children are encouraged to make up oral sentences using the word in other subjects throughout the week.
- When a new word has been introduced and is understood, it is moved from the front of the classroom into the class's display of historic suave words they have learnt.
- All children are reminded about the other recent suave words from the current term or year whenever they write. They are asked if they can create an opportunity to use one or two.
- All teachers should be alert to opportunities across all subjects to revisit and include past suave words as well as the latest one.
- All the class celebrate when a child uses the new suave word of the week in speech or writing.
- All the class celebrate when a child uses any historic suave words in talk or writing.
- All teachers should be familiar with all previous suave words of the week (many schools display them on all classroom walls) and should praise and celebrate children's use of them.
- All staff should know what the suave word of the week is and weave it into their daily interactions and conversations with children.
- Play suave word class champions at the end of the week *(see page 37)*.
- If it is a whole-school or key-stage initiative, play suave word school champions in the following week's assembly *(see page 35)*.
- There are a wide range of resources, games and activities that can support the teaching of suave words *(see page 39)*.

How Do We Teach Pupils with EAL?

When teaching children in the first stages of learning English, all best EAL practice should be followed as usual.

- When introducing or using new suave words, visual clues should be shown, e.g. pictures, examples etc.
- When the suave word is a verb, mime or action should be used.
- When two or more speakers of the same first language are in the same class, time should be allowed for discussion between them in first language to embed the new word in first language.
- If one child with EAL already understands working English, ask them if there is a word in their home language that means the same thing. The Internet is also a good source for translation in all languages. E.g. **angst** is **qalaq** in Arabic and **niepokój** in Polish. Ask the child to help you all with pronunciation and let the whole class say it three times:

qalaq means **angst** in Arabic

qalaq means **angst** in Arabic

qalaq means **angst** in Arabic

- Using translations of the suave words into other languages is not with the intention of teaching other languages but rather as a fun activity and to support the inclusion of children in the early stages of learning English.
- If possible, displays should include translations of new suave words in first language. Parents and community leaders can be a great help with this process if there are no bilingual / multilingual members of staff.

In classrooms and schools with children new to English, providing a translation or a synonym of the suave word in the child's or the class's first language is an important support. Introducing quick questions into many of the games can be fun for all children as well as supportive to those new to English.

- What is **toil** in Urdu? **mehanat**; in Spanish? **el esfuerzo**; in Ukrainian? **vaschkarobota**.
- Which of our suave words translates to the Spanish **el esfuerzo**? It means **effort** or **toil**.
- Can anyone remember the Mandarin for **wary** or **cautious** – **jinshen** so that Da Wei knows what we are talking about?
- Filip, can you remember which of these two words – **toil** or **hoist** means **podnosić** in Polish? It means **hoist**.
- Here are three words in Arabic. Can anyone help Aisha to remember which one means **chaos**? – **fawda**.

There are around 7,000 languages in this world and we should embrace and celebrate every one of them. I have been extremely fortunate to teach children of many cultures and languages including the teaching of hundreds of children who, although highly articulate and confident in several languages, were new to English.

Whether we like it or not, English has become one of the most widely used languages around the world. This doesn't mean that English is superior. We must acknowledge that a large part of the spread of English was due to colonialism which is deeply regrettable. However, it is important that there is a common language to enable effective global communication and connection.

We have a duty to enable children to code switch (move) smoothly and successfully between their own dialects and languages and Standard English, thus giving them the tools to make their own choices and to succeed in a changing world.

What Should We Watch Out For?

There will be a period of instability for many children whenever we teach something new and significant that requires deep understanding and practise. Some children are eager to master the new learning. They may misuse a word for a short time until they have come to full understanding. Other children prefer to remain silent and avoid using a word until they are totally sure they understand it. This is true both for children with EAL learning in English for the first time and for English-speaking children meeting new learning for the first time. It is the same with the learning of suave words.

Teachers will hear and see suave words misused, overused and misspelt. These are not reasons to abandon the process. Just as when children get their first efforts at long multiplication or fractions wrong, teachers will reteach and model, the same best practice is required here.

Common Considerations

- Some children will mispronounce the new suave words at first. This is normal. Praise and correct politely and pleasantly, model frequently and ask the child and class to repeat the word regularly.
- Slight changes in emphasis from a child speaking in a local accent is not a mispronunciation. For example: Do you say *scon* or *scone*? Both are considered correct.
- Some children will use new suave words incorrectly. For example, they may use a noun as a verb, they may use it in the wrong context or as though the meaning is different. Praise for trying to use it and keep modelling and asking the class to make up oral sentences and share.

E.g. A child may say,

> I am **angst** about swimming.

You say,

> Well done, Benny, for trying to use **angst**. It is alright to feel **angst** about swimming.

We might all say,

> I am feeling **angst** about swimming.

- Use the *imaginary friend's* paragraph (with suave words used incorrectly) for children to spot the misused words and suggest what they should have been *(see page 41)*.
- Some children will use far too many suave words in sentences and paragraphs. Praise and demonstrate on an anonymous piece, made up by yourself or the *imaginary friend*, how too many sophisticated words can be worse than none because it makes the paragraph harder to read and can hide the meaning.
- Some children may have learnt most of the suave words but still not use them in their writing. Keep reading out examples of use written by other children and praising them. Use the *imaginary friend's* paragraph with no suave words in, asking the class to insert one or two suave words. If needed, sit with the child and – working together – identify where one or two suave words could be inserted into their last piece of writing.
- Some children will struggle to learn the spelling of new, complex or irregular words. If they are struggling, use a proven spelling system.
- Some children will just use the wrong suave word in a context because they want to use an impressive word but do not yet understand appropriate usage. Praise them for trying to use it and keep modelling.

- Keep asking the class to make up oral sentences and share. Use the *imaginary friend's* paragraph for children to spot the misused words and suggest what they should have been.

Remember

- Continue to revisit previous suave words so that those children who remain uncertain of meanings and appropriate usage have more opportunities to embed them.
- Create as many opportunities to use suave words across the wider curriculum as possible, so that meanings are better understood.
- Regularly remind children that one or two suave words in a paragraph are usually more effective than a significant number.
- Remind children that interspersing simple sentences and / or short sentences amongst longer and more complex sentences can be very powerful.
- Not all children need to know all new words. Variety is good.
- Teaching a rich range of vocabulary is not about prescription. It is about giving children the tools to make their own choices when expressing themselves.

How Do We Maximise Children's Learning Time?

Besides planning for the introduction and use of new suave words, and the ongoing embedding of previous suave words within lessons, there are many opportunities across the school week for further focus on the revisiting and purposeful use of new vocabulary.

Within the school day there are frequently short periods of time that could be maximised for the embedding and understanding of suave words.

These **gaps** of a few minutes or more are ideal for quick suave word of the week revisits – to say the word, spell it and restate the meaning or quick games of **make me up** (*see page 39*) to use the latest suave word.

Making the Most of the Time When:

- One lesson finishes a little earlier than expected and the next lesson is not due to begin for a few minutes.
- Arriving at specialist facilities such as music rooms, IT suites, the hall, gymnasium or changing rooms. Games can be played as the children are lined up outside waiting.
- The lesson is finished, and the teacher is waiting for a colleague to take over.
- A class has to walk in line along corridors or outside. You could use the rhythm of their marching strides.
- The class are unable to go outside for playtime, due to the weather.
- Children's concentration may lapse, or they may benefit from a brain break in longer lessons.

How Do We Teach Across the Curriculum?

In most primary schools and, increasingly, in the first year of secondary school, many or all subjects of the curriculum are taught by the same teacher – the class teacher. This provides the ideal opportunities for revisiting the meanings of suave words already taught, and for using them purposefully in a range of contexts across the curriculum.

Specialist teachers should also be aware of the suave word of the week and should create opportunities to use and embed the word in their subjects.

The teaching of new vocabulary enhances performance and achievement in all subjects. It is not purely the domain of specialist English teachers.

Things to Consider

- Teaching or creating opportunities for use of suave words across the curriculum does not require the changing of existing plans.
- All teachers for the years involved in the programme should be aware of the suave word of the week, including specialist teachers who may not be directly involved with the teaching of language or English.
- Ideally, all teachers should be informed of the new suave word for the upcoming week shortly before the end of the previous week at the very latest.
- Best practice would be the pre-publishing of all suave words for the upcoming half term or term, with distribution to all staff.
- Specialist teachers of subjects other than English should be given time to consult the English or class teachers for advice on implementation, if they so wish.

- All teachers and support staff of all subjects should study their short-term plans for the forthcoming week and decide where they can work in opportunities for the suave word of the week, and how they will address it.
- Display-versions of the suave word of the week could be produced and distributed to all specialist teaching facilities. They could be clearly displayed at the main teaching point as a prompt for staff and children during specialist lessons (you may choose to use the provided resources on our website).
- The subject teacher identifies opportunities to use the new word in that subject's lessons.
- The subject teacher inserts the word naturally in teacher input at the opening and closing of lessons, class discussions and ensuing writing if the content allows.
- Opportunities for revisits and embedding of the suave word of the week will arise most often in class discussions, teacher input and any written work produced by either staff or pupils within any subject under study.
- Staff should alert pupils if they have created opportunities for the suave word. They should encourage a **fastest hands first** or **fastest shout first** system for pupils to indicate awareness of the word's use when they hear or see it (*see page 40*).

Using a Suave Word Across the Curriculum

toil – a verb meaning to work very hard.

Identify whether the word is being used as a verb, noun, adjective or adverb. If there is more than one use, decide as a team whether children need to know all the uses when they first meet a new word.

Using Toil in Different Subjects

- Mathematics – I realise that in these early stages the solving of this problem is a bit of a **toil**, however...
- History – Building an igloo as a family home required several hours of the Inuit's **toil** to shape the wind-blown snow.
- Geography – The Inuit may **toil** all day, hunting for fish through a small hole in thick ice, to feed their families.
- Science – The spider may **toil** for an hour every day to create a new web, as webs do not last.
- PE – I know putting all this away neatly is a bit of a **toil**, but let's see if we can do it in three minutes.
- Art – Many artists **toil** for long hours to achieve the effect they are looking for, and we should not assume that we can finish a piece in a one-hour session.
- Music – Often practising scales can seem like tedious **toil**, but I assure you it will bring its rewards.
- Design and Technology – Sometimes, sanding the surface to get it perfect can feel like endless **toil**, but you will be proud of the result.
- MFL – Reciting the verb *To be* may be a **toil**, but by the end of the week you will know it and it will never be forgotten.

Using Different Forms of Toil

- History – The Roman soldiers were **toiling** for many years to build England's first important road to the north nearly 2000 years ago.
- Geography – Farmers **toiled** for many hours when ploughing their fields using oxen in the past, but now they are being used again on small farms in the USA.
- Science – A mole **toils** non-stop to build new tunnels.
- MFL – The learning of these new French verbs will be hard **toil**.

Suitable Topics for Toil

- History – battles and wars, life in the past anywhere, indigenous peoples in the past, exploration, inventions, creation of transport networks, national and international disasters, major events, famous people.
- Geography – life in other countries, wildlife of other countries, indigenous peoples of other lands, communication systems, industry across the UK / Europe, transport systems, rainforests, conservation, pollution, natural disasters.
- Science – life cycles, life of a species, habitats, human physiology, diet, botany, materials, changes of state, conservation, pollution, preparation for any investigation or experiment.
- PE – learning new skills, playing an intense game, endurance exercises such as long distance running; fielding or defending in some circumstances, setting up / taking down / clearing equipment.
- Art – the work of a particular artist or artisan, preparation and management of materials, execution of stages requiring intense concentration, setting up, clearing away.
- Music – preparation and clearing away, playing scales, repetitive practices, struggling to learn a new technique or piece.
- Design and Technology – preparation and clearing away, working to learn new techniques, working to achieve a finish or effect, working with large or heavy materials, meticulous installations.
- MFL – learn a synonym in the language being taught and use it, repetitive verb exercises, challenging translations.

When launching the suave word of the week, consider the make up of your class. Think about whether the word or associated contexts could be sensitive and handle any issues with great care.

How Do We Track Pupil Progress?

The following are useful points relevant to tracking pupils' progress in learning suave words:

- Games and activities that have not been played for a few weeks or more, and that use historic suave words.
- Improving writing from the *imaginary friend* (see page 41) by changing two or three words to suave synonyms.
- Changing words in their own writing to suave synonyms during the proofing process.

The true measure of a pupil's total understanding and recall of suave words is when they use them naturally and spontaneously in talk or in writing.

Schools must ensure that teaching provides wide opportunities for pupil talk, discussion and input.

Public speaking is also a key opportunity for pupils to demonstrate clear, confident use of appropriate suave words in contexts.

Independent Writing

To be sure that a pupil is using suave words independently and spontaneously, it is important that they frequently write independently. If possible, at least once a week.

For manageability, this could be across the curriculum, thus saving on English subject time on the timetable.

An exemplar schedule for this might be:
- Week 1: English – narrative
- Week 2: History – diary item
- Week 3: Science – report
- Week 4: Geography – information text
- Week 5: Design and Technology – instructions
- Week 6: English – narrative

These pieces need not all be the length of a piece expected in an English lesson, but they should all be done to the same standard, so giving a purpose for this writing is very important.

For example:
- Week 7: PE – match report / governors
- Week 8: History – explanation text / King
- Week 9: Art – biography of Vincent Van Gogh / gallery
- Week 10: Geography – report / newspaper

These pieces should not have had lengthy teacher input and no vocabulary should have been suggested, but – as is always best practice – the teacher should start the activity with a statement reminding pupils that they will be looking for evidence that they have understood and can use their recent learning in writing skills, as well as examining the content of the piece.

Praise and credit should be given in feedback for evidence of attempts to use suave words and for successful and impactful use of suave words. This should be shared with the class.

The teacher may want to keep examples of good evidence in a folder. Each pupil could have a named pocket.

Parents and other visitors will find looking at a particular pupil's pocket of writing samples most interesting and helpful.

What Is Suave Word Homework?

Not all schools will have a homework policy. However, due to the increasing importance of promoting extended talk in homes, we do recommend that all schools invest in suave word homework. It is always enjoyable and is a totally talk-led activity. It may not have the title **homework** in some schools, if that would be contrary to best interests. The teacher could just say,

> I want you to take this home and ask your family to do it with you.

> There are lots of activity resources on our website that can be used at home.
> **www.RosWilsonEd.com/free**

For most children, this homework will be once a week on the day the new suave word is launched, which is usually the first day of the week. In many schools, older children may have a second, subject-related word around the middle of the week.

It is important to explain suave word homework to all parents, preferably before it is introduced to children. When parents first attend school to enrol their children there is usually an introductory session to explain routines etc. This can be a good opportunity for the explanation.

Using Suave Word Homework

- The importance of talk and vocabulary should be explained to parents. They should be asked to consider how they can arrange busy schedules to sit down together with their children to discuss the new suave word, using it in sentences they make up together.

- Because many families may have more than one child in school, the whole school suave word of the week should, ideally, be the same word. Using the same word for all children will make their conversations so much more manageable and focused.
- This is when short words are helpful to cater for different ages in one family.
- Longer suave words are easier for young children when they are made up of a root word they already know with a prefix or suffix e.g. **tasteful** or are made up of two short words they know e.g. **songbird**.
- At some point in the day the new suave word of the week is launched, possibly at the beginning or end of the English lesson or in a plenary at the end of the day. Teachers will give out suave word homework slips or send home a message in the school's preferred way. They should read through the message with their class before the children go home. This enables the child to read the message back to their family.
- Messages say something like:

> My homework tonight is to talk with you using our new suave word **wary**. This means cautious and a bit nervous. Can I say when I feel a bit **wary**? Can you say when you feel **wary**? Can we make up some sentences using **wary**? Thank you.

- Alternatively, teachers could use the free suave word homework resource from our website.
- Older children may have a second suave word each week, usually given out in the middle of the week. This may be more complex and is often relevant to subject matter under study; for example **anxious** or **anguish** when studying the fate of the animal population of a forest when bush fires spread.
- Families could do suave word homework while they are eating their evening meal together and they should make it fun. This could be included in the message, or they could be told at parents' evening.

- Families should remember that any time they are together for social time they could turn off their technology and enjoy a chat using some of their new suave words, for example:
  - At any meal at home or when eating out.
  - In the doctor's waiting room.
  - While going round the supermarket.
  - While out for a walk.
  - While travelling to or from school or on longer journeys.
  - Before or during bedtime story.
- There are a wide range of suave word homework resources on our website. They can be used on other nights of the week to reinforce the learning of the new word or can be sent out some weeks later as a refresher activity. They can be printed off or shared digitally, discussed with the class and sent home as they are presented.

Remember

- The more often a child talks about the new word and uses it in new contexts, the more quickly they will learn it.
- When parents talk about the word and use it, it refreshes their memory or teaches them it too.
- Parents and children can have fun using the word as often as they can and watch out for each other using it.

What Is Suave Word Assembly?

Suave word assembly would ideally take place on the first day of the school week or – at the latest – on the second day. It is usually a whole key stage in large schools and whole school if the accommodation allows. In some schools it may be a year group assembly.

The atmosphere should be cheerful and fun, with all children encouraged to participate when appropriate. It may conclude with the exciting suave word school champion contest.

Leading the Assembly

- Suave word assembly is the celebration of the suave words from previous weeks and the launch of the new suave word of the week.
- To be the launch of the new suave word of the week, the assembly will ideally take place on the first day of the week or as early as possible.
- The assembly should also be a lively and fun celebration of the previous several weeks' suave words, with children and staff giving examples of how they have used them.
- The lead teacher could fire the historic suave words at all the children or at named classes, and the children call out the spelling, or the meaning or a synonym.
- The assembly might contain one or two fun games and activities *(see page 46)*.
- The assembly might include a competition called suave word school champions which is described later in this section.

- The assembly usually concludes with the launch of the new suave word which should be introduced both in writing and orally.
  - The lead teacher or head should lead the school in saying the new word together, loudly, clearly and correctly, three times.
  - They should then all say and spell it.
  - The leader then gives the definition and an example of how to use the word.
  - If there is enough time, the children could then make up one or two sentences using the word but, as this will all be repeated back in the classroom, it is not essential.

Suave Word School Champions

Suave word school champions can be played at the end of suave word assembly, just before the new suave word of the week is launched.

- The lead teacher calls out each Suave Word Class Champion (*see page 37*) one by one and they are all clapped as they come out and line up across the stage.
- Everyone plays two or three suave word games that the classes have been playing recently, using historic suave words from previous weeks in different sentences or tasks.
- Each child gets a question in turn.
- As a child answers correctly, they step forward and are clapped.
- If the answer is wrong, the next child is asked.
- The winners are counted and the two children who won the most questions are in the play-off.
- The two winners now play the same games with the previous week's suave word in new contexts.
- The winner is the Suave Word School Champion of the week and wins a book or pen or similar appropriate prize.
- All the Suave Word Class Champions are given a certificate.

What Is Suave Word Class Champions?

Suave word class champions is played in classrooms on the last day of the school week. It may be a fun activity for each class alone, or it may be played to identify a Champion to go forward to the next suave word assembly. The suave word school champions play-off takes place after everyone has enjoyed participating in quick, fun suave word activities in assembly *(see page 35)*.

How to Play

Recycle a list of between five and ten (depending on age) previous suave words. That week's suave word should always be first of the chosen words for the game. Everyone should use all the activities below to ensure that whichever ones children are challenged with in assembly, they will be confident in having a go.

- The teacher calls out a suave word and the fastest to shout the spelling correctly scores a point.
- The teacher calls out a suave word and the fastest to shout the definition scores a point.
- The teacher calls out a suave word and the fastest to shout the word **sentence** can answer with a full sentence using the word. If the word is used correctly, they score a point.
- The teacher puts three short sentences on the board and calls out a suave word. The fastest to shout **one**, **two** or **three** to identify the correct sentence it could be used in scores a point.
- The teacher puts three words on the board and calls out a suave word. The fastest to shout the correct synonym scores a point.
- These games may be repeated in random order using new contexts.

The child with the most points is the week's Suave Word Class Champion and earns a certificate.

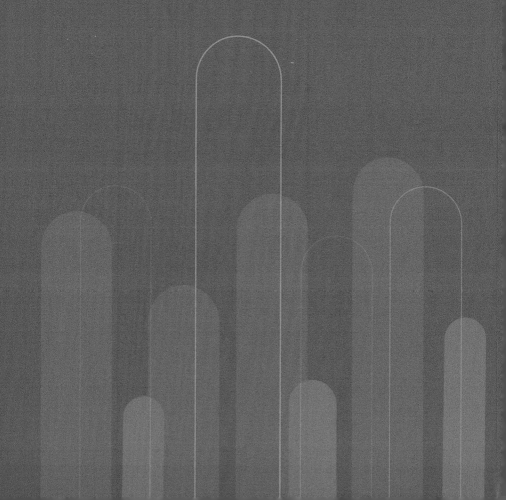

SECTION TWO
GAMES AND ACTIVITIES

What Activities Can We Use?

Use general talking activities across the curriculum to teach and revisit suave words, definitions and synonyms. For example through group discussions, brainstorming, ways to share or generate ideas, summarisation of lesson objectives, conclusion of lessons, evaluation and appraisal.

In classrooms and schools with children new to English, providing a translation or a synonym in first language is an important support *(see page 20)*.

These ideas are ideal for use in any subject or context. Further ideas are exemplified in the suave word resources section *(see page 46)*. All activities should be light-hearted, fun and played at a brisk speed.

Make Me Up

The teacher fires quick topics at the class or group and they make up one or more sentences about that topic, incorporating the target suave word. This may also be played with children in twos, threes or larger groups, with children taking it in turns to call out a potential subject. E.g.

Teacher: *Make me up* a sentence about our last PE lesson, using the word **toil**.

Child: It was hard **toil** putting all the apparatus away when we were tired at the end of the lesson.

Teacher: *Make me up* a sentence about something you did yesterday, using the word **wary**.

Child: I tried to play with our new puppy, but he was **wary** of me.

Fastest Shout First

The teacher fires quick challenges at the class and names the fastest to shout the correct answer. This game is ideal for the finding of the Suave Word Class Champion *(see page 37)*. E.g.

> *Fastest shout first*, the suave word that means **cautious**.

> *Fastest shout first*, the spelling of the suave word **wary**.

> *Fastest shout first*, the meaning of the suave word **toil**.

> *Fastest shout first*, the word in the paragraph that is not used correctly.

> *Fastest shout first*, a synonym for the suave word **abrupt**.

> *Fastest shout first*, an antonym (the opposite meaning) for the suave word **loath**.

> *Fastest shout first*, a suave word used in this sentence or paragraph.

> *Fastest shout first*, a sentence using the suave word **resist**.

All the above activities could be used for the same word in one session if, for example, it is the new suave word or one they might find very helpful in upcoming work.

Fastest Finger First

The teacher calls out a challenge at the class and identifies the child who pointed to the correct answer first. E.g.

Fastest finger first, point to **wary** in the dictionary.

Fastest finger first, point to a synonym for **wary** in the thesaurus.

Fastest finger first, point to **wary** in the second paragraph on this page.

Fastest finger first, point to the best synonym on the screen for **wary**.

Fastest finger first, point to the correct definition for **wary** on your handout.

Fastest finger first, point to the word that is spelt incorrectly on your screens.

Fastest finger first, point to a suave word that our imaginary friend, Bud, has used incorrectly.

The Imaginary Friend

An empty chair is provided for the imaginary friend. This fictitious member of the class makes the mistakes other class members make. They are used as an opportunity for children to correct their errors and learn from them.

The imaginary friend protects the class from the embarrassment of being identified for making mistakes. He protects their self-esteem. Children really enjoy the potential for humour – many teachers **talk** to the empty chair sometimes, and even **accept answers** from **him** when no one else offers an answer.

It is a good idea to make the imaginary friend a boy, so that he can be used as a positive role model when appropriate. The teacher should choose an appropriate name for the profile of the class, which should also be a name that is extremely unlikely to be heard in the school. E.g.

Where has Bud used a word incorrectly?

Bud has used some super vocabulary in this paragraph. Tell your friends which words you particularly like.

Where has Bud misspelt a suave word?

Where could Bud have inserted a suave word?

What has Bud used too many of in this paragraph?

Bud has used **said** five times in this paragraph, what synonyms might he have used?

Bud has created a wonderful sentence here. Why do you think I especially liked it?

Bud has used far too many suave words here – which ones could we change into simpler synonyms?

Dictionary Game

All class members should be given dictionaries or share them one between two. These should be dictionaries suitable for the location of suave words. Some children's dictionaries only contain a very narrow range of quite basic vocabulary. E.g.

> *Fastest finger first* for the following suave word in the dictionary. Ready? **Wary**.

> Well done, Joseph, now all read the definition out together.

> What part of speech does it say it might be?

> Does anyone know a synonym for **wary**?

> Now let's play *make me up* with **wary**.

> And again: *fastest finger first* for the following suave word. Ready? **Toil**.

Or:

> *Fastest shout first*, the definition of the word **lure**.

> Well done, Lina, now *fastest shout first*, a synonym for **lure**.

> Now let's play *make me up* with **lure**.

Thesaurus Game

All class members should be given a thesaurus or share them one between two. E.g.

> **Fastest finger first** for the following suave word in the thesaurus. Ready? **Wary.**

> Well done, Francesca, now all read the synonyms out together.

> Who can remember the meaning of **wary?**

> Does anyone know an antonym (a word that means the opposite of) for **wary?**

> Now let's play **make me up** with **wary.**

> And again: **fastest finger first** for the following suave word. Ready? **Omit.**

Suave Word Circles

Version 1

Seat children in circles of around six.

- The teacher calls out a suave word and gives the challenge, e.g. give a definition, or synonym or spell it.
- The group agree an answer and try to be the fastest to shoot their hands up.
- Within each group, children take it in turns to be the fastest to shout the answer to the class, and their group clap or cheer.

Seat children in circles of around six.

- Place a set of suave word cards *(see page 51)* in the centre of each circle, shuffled and all face down.
- Each child takes a card in turn and reads it out loud, keeping it hidden to hide the spelling.
- The children in the group all say the word out loud clearly.
- Children round the circle spell the word out loud – one letter per child – starting with the child on the card's left.
- The child with the card says whether this was correct or not and returns the card to the bottom of the pile.
- The next child takes a card, and the game is repeated.

The suave word cards can be downloaded for free from our website.
www.RosWilsonEd.com/free

What Are the Suave Word Resources?

There are a wide range of suave word resources available for free on our website. We are adding more all the time.

Teachers in schools that are not following the suave word programme are still welcome to avail themselves of these resources and to use them with their classes as they see fit.

Our intention is that new suave words should be introduced to a class, a year, a key stage or a whole school in a planned and agreed approach that is understood by everyone involved.

Everyone should feel free to use these ideas to create their own resources, making up games and activities using words and rules of their own choice.

These resources could be used a second time a few weeks later, as homework activities or as quick classroom refreshers.

These resources can be downloaded for free from our website.
www.RosWilsonEd.com/free

Suave Word of the Week

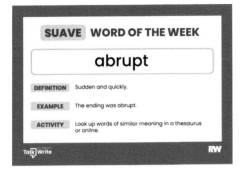

SUAVE WORD OF THE WEEK

abrupt

DEFINITION	Sudden and quickly.
EXAMPLE	The ending was abrupt.
ACTIVITY	Look up words of similar meaning in a thesaurus or online.

Talk)Write   RW

This resource can be displayed at the front of the classroom for the whole week that it is the target suave word. It is usually the first resource to be used when launching a new suave word. At the end of the week, it would be added to the display of previous words of the week.

The following are the types of activities the teacher would lead (usually in English lessons but supported by re-enforcement activities across the curriculum) in introducing and embedding the new suave word:

- All read the suave word **abrupt** together.
- All say the meaning of **abrupt**.
- All play *make me up* to use **abrupt** in a sentence about something the class are currently learning or talking about. (For example: The Santa Maria's adventures on the oceans came to an **abrupt** end.)
- All give the definition of **abrupt**.
- All read this exemplar **abrupt** sentence together.
- All say what happens or what the meaning is in this exemplar sentence with **abrupt** in.
- All use a thesaurus (or brainstorm) to identify synonyms for **abrupt**, e.g. **sudden hurried hasty blunt**
- Play *make me up* new sentences using **abrupt**.
- Can you all spell **abrupt**?
- Play the games and activities in the many resources for **abrupt** over the following weeks.

For a full description of teaching suave words, *see page 14.*

Suave Word Assembly

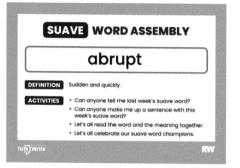

This resource can be used to support the launch of a new suave word in assembly. Dedicate a whole-school, key-stage or year assembly to become a weekly suave word assembly. This should, ideally, take place on the first day of the week (or as soon as possible).

- It should start with fast, fun activities to revisit the suave words previously learnt that term or year by all children present.
- It could then be used to celebrate the Suave Word Class Champions (if adopted) *(see page 37)*.
- It could then be used to play-off the Class Champions to identify the Suave Word School Champion.
- The launch of the new suave word usually comes at the close of this assembly.

For a full description of the suave word assembly, *see page 35*.

You could use this resource as a model to make similar resources using the class's own suave words.

Suave Word Homework

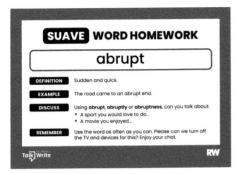

This resource supports the first evening's homework (you may decide not to use the word *homework*) for a new suave word. It may be used in the first week of the launch of the new suave word, or a few weeks later to refresh. It may be used as many times as is needed to embed the content.

In School

- This resource is usually used in class at the close of the day on which the new suave word is launched.
- The teacher usually goes through the wording on this homework resource to ensure the children understand what they are being asked to do.

> What does it mean? Does it have more than one meaning? Which one are we using today?

> Can you explain what happened to the road ahead?

- Discuss the activity to be done at home with the family, without doing it. For example,

> What sort of things might you talk about?

> What do you think your family might say?

- Play *make me up* using **abrupt**:
  - *Make me up* a sentence about the end of the war using **abrupt**.
  - *Make me up* a sentence about a cross child using **abrupt**.
  - *Make me up* a sentence about a sudden change in the weather using **abrupt**.

At Home

- The child or children read through the homework resource with their family.
- They discuss what their teacher said and did with them.
- They do each of the activities together as a family.
- Throughout the evening – and the rest of the week – the family try to use the new suave word as often as they can.
- Every week the family try to use historic suave words from previous weeks as often as possible.
- Older children may also receive a second, more challenging word later in the week. Remember to include this in your conversations.

For a full description of suave word homework, *see page 32.*

You could use this resource as a model to make similar resources using the class's own suave words.

Suave Word Cards

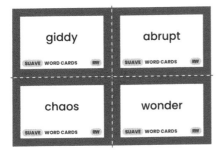

These sets of 32 cards use a range of our suave words to enable games and activities. There are endless ways to have fun and reinforce suave words using these cards.

Suave Word Snap

This game can be played by up to four children in a group.

- Make matching sets of cards.
- Shuffle two matching sets together.
- Put the pile face down in the middle of the table.
- Each child turns a card in turn and places it on a new pile at the side, face up.
- If a newly-turned card matches the previous one, children shout *SNAP*.
- The fastest to shout has won and the game either continues or the cards are shuffled and it starts again.

Suave Word Match Me

This game can be played in two or threes.

- Shuffle two matching sets and place them all over the tabletop face down.
- Shuffle them around some more.
- A child turns a card, shows it and all the group read the word aloud.

- The child turns it back down in its place.
- The next child turns another card, shows it and all the group read the word aloud.
- The child turns it back down in its place.
- Continue until a child turns a card they think matches one that has already been turned. They have to remember where the other card was and turn it over too. If the two cards match, the child keeps both. If it doesn't, both cards are put back, face down.
- The game continues until all the cards have been matched.
- The child with the most pairs of winning matches has won.
- You can vary the difficulty by using a different number of cards.

Other Games

- The teacher shows a word from a shuffled pile for **fastest shout first**.
- Use enough matching sets for a set between two or three. The teacher calls a synonym and the fastest to find the actual word and show / shout it out wins.
- Pupils in twos or threes shuffle and divide the pack evenly between them. They either:
    - take it in turns to show a card and the other must shout the meaning,
    - read the word from the card and the other must spell it,
    - show a card and the other must use it in a sentence, or
    - show a card and the other must give a synonym.

You could use this resource as a model to make similar resources using the class's own suave words.

Suave Word Synonyms

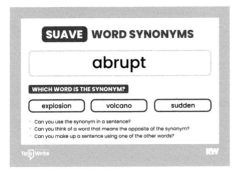

This resource shows three possible synonyms for a suave word, with one being correct. It may be used in the first week of the launch of the new suave word, or a few weeks later in lessons or as homework to refresh. It may be used as many times as is needed to embed the content.

- Refresh or teach what the word *synonym* means if the children need it: a word that means the same or almost the same as another word.
- Read the three options and decide which is the synonym for **abrupt**.
- Think of a word that means the opposite to the word at the top. The opposite to **abrupt** might be **slow** or **slowly** depending on the way **abrupt** was used.
- Use one of the two words that are not synonyms to make up a new sentence about something else. E.g.
    - The fireworks sounded like a huge **explosion**.
    - I saw a **volcano** erupting in the video.
- We have often chosen the incorrect synonym options because they are synonyms of words that sound a bit like or are related to the suave word. In this example, one of the incorrect options is **explosion** because **abrupt** sounds a bit like **erupt**. As confidence grows, you may be able to have fun with this and ask pupils to see if they can spot these choices.

You could use this resource as a model to make similar resources using the class's own suave words.

Suave Word Scramble

This resource has a scrambled suave word that must be unscrambled. It should ideally be used within the first week of introduction of the new suave word. It could then be replicated with different combinations of the letters to re-enforce the correct spelling.

- Spell out the scrambled word together, the way it is written in the yellow box. E.g. r u p b t a
- Can anyone guess what the suave word is straight away?
- Read the clue and discuss in twos or threes. Can you now find the suave word?
- Teach the **circle** technique. Put the scrambled letters into a circle to make spotting the actual word easier. Be careful with repeated letters.

- If children are struggling, give the first letter of the word. Then the second, if needed.
- Play **make me up** a sentence with the word **abrupt** in it.
- Does anyone remember a synonym for the word **abrupt**?

You could use this resource as a model to make similar resources using the class's own suave words.

Suave Word Select

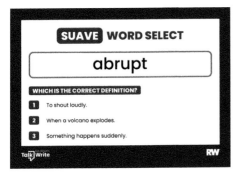

This resource shows three possible definitions for a suave word with one being correct. It should ideally be used within the first week of introduction of the new suave word. It could be used as many times as is needed to embed the definition.

- Read the word **abrupt** together.
- Read the three possible definitions.
- Which one of them is the correct definition for **abrupt**?
- *Make me up* a sentence using the suave word **abrupt** (it does not matter if the sentences are similar to ones made up previously).
- Can you find a suave word for each of the other two definitions? E.g. **bellow** for *To shout loudly.* Or **erupt** for *When a volcano explodes.*
- Do you know a synonym for **abrupt**? E.g. **sudden**.
- Can you use the suave words relating to the other two definitions in sentences about something the class are currently learning.

You could use this resource as a model to make similar resources using the class's own suave words.

Suave Word Sense

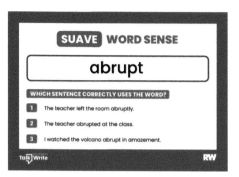

This resource shows three sentences with one using a suave word correctly. It should ideally be used within the first week of introduction of the new suave word. It could be replicated with different sets of sentences to further embed the correct word.

- Read the suave word **abrupt** together.
- Refresh the definition of **abrupt**.
- Read all three sentences together.
- Refresh the spelling of **abrupt**.
- Play *fastest shout first* to list synonyms for **abrupt**.
- Now reread the three sentences again.
- Children discuss and choose the correct sentence for the use of **abrupt** (sentence one).
- Children could make up three sentences in similar style for their peers to repeat the exercise.
- Discuss and substitute a synonym for those that are incorrect in the other two sentences.

> You could use this resource as a model to make similar resources using the class's own suave words.

Suave Word Sentences

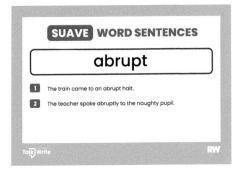

This resource shows the different forms of a suave word as sentences and meanings change. It can be used any time after pupils have developed understanding of the meaning of the word. It could be used as many times as is needed for the children to embed the words.

It may be used purely as a visual aid for teaching this point, or as a prompt on the suave word wall. It could also be used as an activity:

- Read through the sentences.
- Discuss how the changing of the sentences means that a different form of the word is needed.
- Put a new sentence on the screen and give pupils a new suave word that they already know.
- Ask pupils whether they need to change the form of the word to insert it into the sentence.
- Complete the sentence by inserting the word.
- Give the class two or three new sentences that require the word form to change.
- Ask them to copy the sentences and insert the correct form of the word.
- Discuss the correct forms and check answers.

You could use this resource as a model to make similar resources using the class's own suave words.

Suave Word Meaning Match

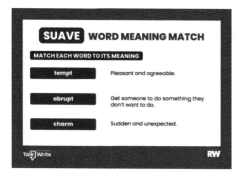

This resource has three different suave words and three definitions to be matched. It is a useful activity for revisiting historic suave words. It could then be replicated with new sets of words. It may be used at any time after the introduction of a new suave word, either as part of the initial embedding process, as a refresher / revisit or as homework.

This resource uses previously learnt suave words and not the current suave word of the week.

- Match the words to their meanings e.g. join the words to their correct meanings with a straight line.
- Make up three or more sentences, using one of the suave words in each sentence. E.g. **tempt abrupt charm**
  - I tried to **tempt** the puppy with a treat.
  - He left the room **abruptly**.
  - The new teacher is **charming**.
- Work in small groups to make up one sentence with all the suave words in.
  - I tried to **tempt** the child with my **charm** but she screamed **abruptly**.
- You may choose to change the form of the suave words (e.g. **charming** rather than **charm**).

You could use this resource as a model to make similar resources using the class's own suave words.

Suave Word Spaces

SUAVE WORD SPACES

INSERT THE CORRECT WORD INTO EACH SENTENCE

| doubt | urge | abrupt |

The angry woman was very .... with me.

I .... I can climb that very steep hill.

He had to .... me to try and climb the hill.

Talk Write   RW

This resource has three different suave words and three sentences with gaps to place the correct suave word. It is a useful activity for revisiting historic suave words. It could then be replicated with new sentences and different suave words. It may be used any time after the launch of a new suave word, either as part of the initial embedding process or as a refresher / revisit to consolidate understanding. This resource uses previously learnt suave words and not the current suave word of the week.

- Read the three suave words in the boxes.
- What do they mean?
- Close your eyes and spell them.
- Give synonyms for each of the three words.
- Read the first sentence. Which word would fit into it to make sense?
- Copy the sentence and put in the word or read it out loud to someone.
- Do the same with the second and third sentences.
- Can you make up your own sentences using the same words?
- Can you use all three words in one sensible sentence? E.g.
  - I **doubt** even your strongest **urging** will stop the angry man speaking so **abruptly**.
- You may choose to change the form of the suave words (e.g. **urging** rather than **urge**).

You could use this resource as a model to make similar resources using the class's own suave words.

Suave Word Spaces Variations

Version 1

- The teacher puts a border of suave words the class have learnt round the outside of the white board or children face the historic suave word display.
- The teacher puts up a sentence in the middle of the board with a missing word – or reads out a sentence with a missing word.
- Children could play:
  - **Fastest shout first** to say which of the suave words is the correct one.
  - Each child in turn, going round the class, says which is the right one.
  - The class is divided in half and the two teams play off against each other.

Version 2

- The teacher puts a sentence with a word missing on the white board.
- The teacher has a pack of suave word cards *(see page 51)*, using only cards the children have already learnt. If these are words not provided in our resources, a member of staff could make playing cards similar to ours.
- The teacher turns the cards and holds them up one at a time and all the class read the word out loud as fast as they can.
- When they meet the card they think is the correct one they shoot their hands up.
- A new sentence appears on the whiteboard.

Suave Word Synonym Match

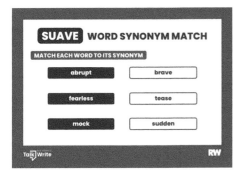

This resource has three different suave words and three synonyms to be matched. It is a useful activity for revisiting historic suave words. It could then be replicated with different suave words. It may be used any time after the launch of a new suave word, either as part of the initial embedding process or as a refresher / revisit to consolidate understanding. This resource uses previously learnt suave words and not the current suave word of the week.

- Read the three words down the left-hand side.
- Read the three words down the right-hand side.
- Match the suave word to its correct synonym. This might be done orally or with a pencil: draw a line to join each correct word to the synonym that matches it.
- Give definitions for all words.
- Call out other synonyms for each of the suave words.
- Call out synonyms for each of the other words.
- Play **make me up** to create sentences with each of the words. Can you make up a sentence with two of the words in – or all three? E.g.
  - Despite my **fearless** try to jump the stream, my friend laughed **abruptly** and then **mocked** me.
- You may choose to change the form of the suave words (e.g. **abruptly** rather than **abrupt**).

You could use this resource as a model to make similar resources using the class's own suave words.

Suave Word Ditty

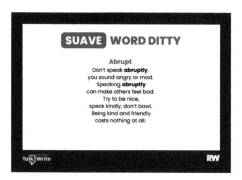

SUAVE WORD DITTY

Abrupt
Don't speak **abruptly**,
you sound angry or mad.
Speaking **abruptly**
can make others feel bad.
Try to be nice,
speak kindly, don't bawl,
Being kind and friendly
costs nothing at all.

Talk Write   RW

Suave word ditties are short jingles. They provide a fun example of the suave word in context for discussion and reinforcement. Children will enjoy reading the suave word ditties aloud with clear diction and expression as well as learning and performing some of them. These are most often introduced in the week of the launch of the new suave word.

- Refresh how to spell **abrupt**.
- What is the meaning of **abrupt**?
- *Make me up* a sentence using **abrupt**.
- Do you all know a synonym for **abrupt**?
- Read the **abrupt** ditty together. Discuss what is happening.
- Which other suave word has been used in line six? – **bawl**.
- Does anyone know what that means? (Cry or shout loudly)
- Working in twos, threes or as a class – can you think of any words that rhyme with **abrupt**? E.g. **stuffed erupt supped**
- Some words are hard to find rhymes for. Check before doing the rhyming activity as it sometimes may be too difficult.
- Read the ditty again.
- Consider writing more lines using the identified rhyming words E.g.
  - Always keep calm, there's no need to **erupt**,
    Nobody likes it, when you are **abrupt**.
- Consider learning some of the ditties.
- Consider making up a new suave word ditty with a recent suave word.
- Use for handwriting practise.

You could use this resource as a model to make similar resources using the class's own suave words.

Suave Word Plus

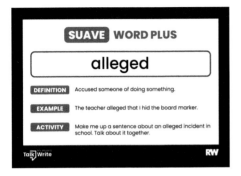

SUAVE WORD PLUS

alleged

DEFINITION Accused someone of doing something.

EXAMPLE The teacher alleged that I hid the board marker.

ACTIVITY Make me up a sentence about an alleged incident in school. Talk about it together.

Talk Write   RW

Suave word plus are suave words that are more complex. They may have more than two syllables. They may have letters that are not making their usual sounds. They may be highly sophisticated. They should be launched around the middle of the week – not at the same time as the whole-school suave word. The resource may be used for homework. **Suave word plus** is aimed at key stage two and above. As ever, you know your class, so use your judgement to decide what your pupils are ready for.

- Read and discuss the definition together.
- Can you *make me up* a sentence using the word **alleged**?
- Read the example. Explain what the sentence means. It is important that children know that the fact that the *trick* is **alleged** means they may not have done it.
- Read the activity and discuss it together. Think of ideas for what the **alleged** incident in school might be. Make up a sentence about one that you like, using the word **alleged**.
- Play *make me up* across the curriculum to use the word in sentences for other subjects.

You could use this resource as a model to make similar resources using the class's own suave words.

All the resources and activities illustrated and explained in this book could be reproduced for use with the *suave word plus* words.

Summary

The ideas and suggestions in this book are intended to support teachers in their journey to expand their pupils' vocabulary, their understanding of ambitious words, the correct usage of them and their ability to both talk and write in rich and descriptive language.

Our profession is composed of adults who are creative thinkers and innovative practitioners. We fully expect that teachers will adapt, extend and emulate the ideas they have found beneficial for their pupils.

A growing awareness of the benefits of an expansive and expressive vocabulary will alert pupils to the pleasures of spotting and seeking out even more suave words as they read, watch movies and interact with technology.

There will be a constant supply of new language that will require explanation and embedding, but children will have favourite games and activities that make this process a fun and rewarding part of every school week.

Finally, teachers who create opportunities for children to develop their public speaking skills and to perform in presentations and productions before various audiences, including sections of their own school, neighbouring schools, the local elderly community and so on, will endow great gifts of oracy that will empower their pupils for life.